CW00349337

The Bags - Copyright © 2007 by Index Book, SL
First published in 2007
Published by: Index Book SL.
C/ Consell de Cent 160 local 3 - 08015 Barcelona
Phone: +34 93 454 5547
Fax: +34 93 454 8438
E-mail: ib@indexbook.com
URL: www.indexbook.com

Author/Graphic Design: Mito Design
Translation: Silvia Guiu
Printing: SNP Leefung Printers (Shenzhen) Co., Ltd
SNP Leefung Printing Building,
N° 1 Nangguang Road, Nanshan Zone,
Shenzhen, P.R.C. - China
Phone: +86-755-86063923
Fax: +86-755-26644223

The BAGS

The captions and artwork in this book are based on material supplied
by the designers whose work is included. No part of this publication
may be reproduced or transmitted in any form or by any means, electronic
or mechanical, including photocopy, recording or any information storage
and retrieval system, without permission in writing from the copyright owner(s).

Printed in China ISBN 978-84-96309-58-6
While every effort has been made to ensure accuracy,
neither Index Book nor the author under any
circumstances accept responsibility
for any errors or omissions.

wmg
and
of
ated

INTRODUCTION

A book about bags? That was the first question from our editor, when we decided to put forth the idea of a book about bags. Living in one of the world's most fashionable cities, we are constantly exposed to dozens of new styles of bags in all different types: plastic, rubber, leather, paper, you name it. Whether woman or man, we just can't live without them.

The idea behind this book was to show you the new, up-and-coming styles and trends, and there's no doubt that you will identify with at least one of the models shown here.

This book will also serve an inspiration to designers of all kinds as they develop models and designs for this oh-so-essential object.

Mito Design

CHAPTERS

DAY

A container of flexible material, such as paper, plastic, or leather, which is used for carrying or storing items.

001   Juarez Escosteguy

:: Day

002   Juarez Escosteguy

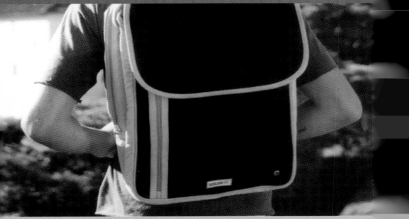

003   Juarez Escosteguy

004

Juarez Escosteguy

005

Juarez Escosteguy

Juarez Escosteguy

:: Day

Juarez Escosteguy

Juarez Escosteguy

010   Pure Evil

011   Pure Evil

Pure Evil

:: Day

drum sling

pvc
coated
screen
printed
rugged
canvas
body
& flap

ballistic
nylon strap

© 2006 VINE360, LLC. All Rights Reserved. www.VINE360.com

Crash Messenger

ribbed
reflective
pvc

screenprinted
rugged canvas
flap and body

ballistic
nylon gusset
and strap

bike chain
for wallet

reflective
tape straps

© 2006 VINE360, LLC. All Rights Reserved. www.VINE360.com

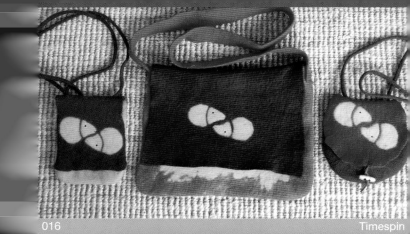

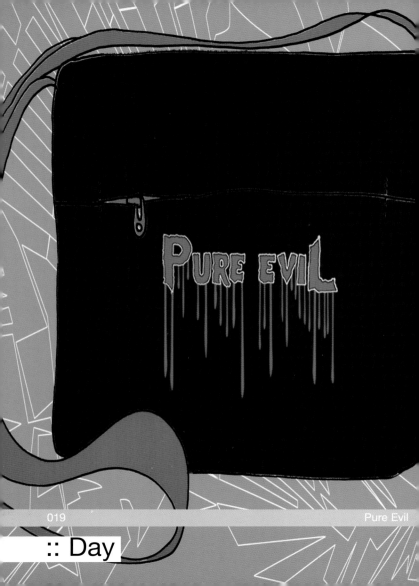

:: Day

020   Pure Evil

021   Pure Evil

Marshall Trading

022 :: 023

025

Arturo Elena

:: Day

Consanguineo

Consanguineo

Consanguineo

Consanguineo

Guilherme Marconi - Cloning

:: Day

Hardtroze

Hardtroze

Hardtroze

:: Day

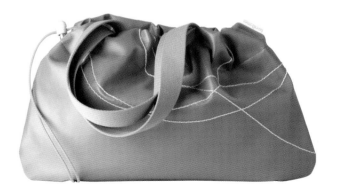

:: Day

Hardtroze

Hardtroze

Ordinarymary

:: Day

Min Agostini

Min Agostini

Min Agostini

046 :: 047

:: Day

062   Roberta Montagnoli

063   Roberta Montagnoli

Roberta Montagnoli

Roberta Montagnoli

:: Day

Story

Story

face messenger

screenprinted
rugged canvas
body & strap

© 2006 VINE360, LLC. All Rights Reserved. www.VINE360.com

thorn sling

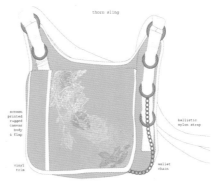

screen
printed
rugged
canvas
body
& flap

vinyl
trim

ballistic
nylon strap

wallet
chain

© 2006 VINE360, LLC. All Rights Reserved. www.VINE360.com

dahlia messenger

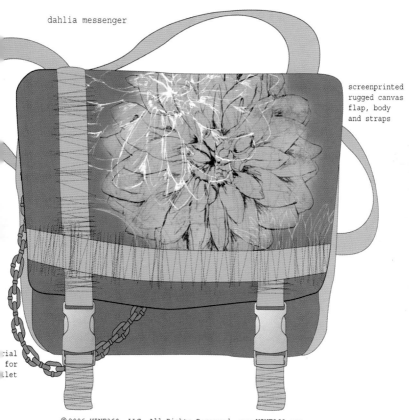

screenprinted
rugged canvas
flap, body
and straps

ial
for
klet

© 2006 VINE360, LLC. All Rights Reserved. www.VINE360.com

054 :: 055

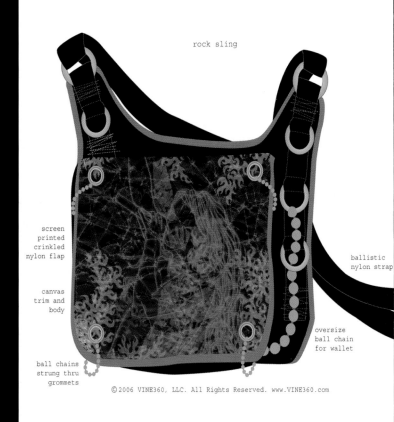

rock sling

screen
printed
crinkled
nylon flap

ballistic
nylon strap

canvas
trim and
body

oversize
ball chain
for wallet

ball chains
strung thru
grommets

©2006 VINE360, LLC. All Rights Reserved. www.VINE360.com

:: Day

surf messenger

screenprinted
rugged canvas
flap and body

ballistic
nylon gusset
and straps

bike chain
for wallet

© 2006 VINE360, LLC. All Rights Reserved. www.VINE360.com

peacock messenger

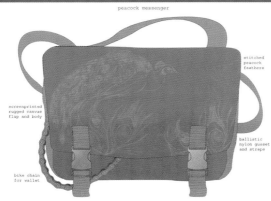

stitched
peacock
feathers

screenprinted
rugged canvas
flap and body

ballistic
nylon gusset
and straps

bike chain
for wallet

© 2006 VINE360, LLC. All Rights Reserved. www.VINE360.com

076   Vivi Tedeschi

077   Vivi Tedeschi

Vivi Tedeschi

058 :: 059

Rico Lins + Studio

:: Day

Alzira & Lucio

Alzira & Lucio

082   Alzira & Lucio

083   Alzira & Lucio

Alzira & Lucio

Vivi Tedeschi

:: Day

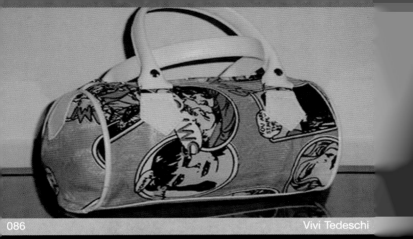

086   Vivi Tedeschi

087   Vivi Tedeschi

Alzira & Lucio

Alzira & Lucio

:: Day

Alzira & Lucio

091   Alzira & Lucio

:: Day

092 Alzira & Lucio

093 Alzira & Lucio

094

095

Mamba Atelier – Karina Moreira Pinto

Carina Stinga

:: Day

098

Carina Stinga

099

Carina Stinga

Mamba Atelier – Karina Moreira Pinto

:: Day

Mamba Atelier – Karina Moreira Pinto

Mamba Atelier – Karina Moreira Pinto

 Naja Conrad

 Naja Conrad

nº 003

Matt Joyce

078 :: 079

:: Day

Carina Stinga

Story

112

113

Rosa Vidal

Rosa Vidal

:: Day

Rosa Vidal

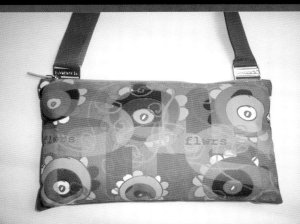

Rosa Vidal

Traumschallplatten

Traumschallplatten

:: Day

Rosa Vidal

086 :: 087

:: Day

Rosa Vidal

Giuseppe Lavicoli

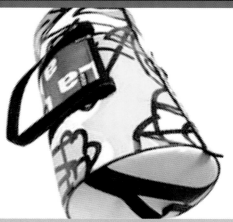

:: Day

Vaho Works

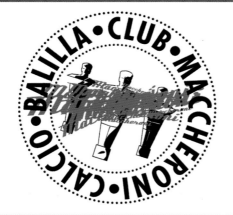

Giuseppe Lavicoli

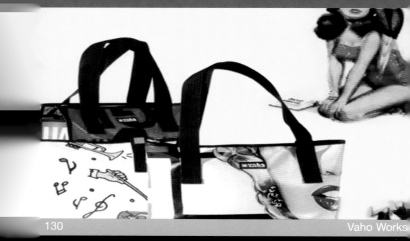

gĭrl pack

1

2

3

1 LULA

3 GALA

4 RITA

094 :: 095

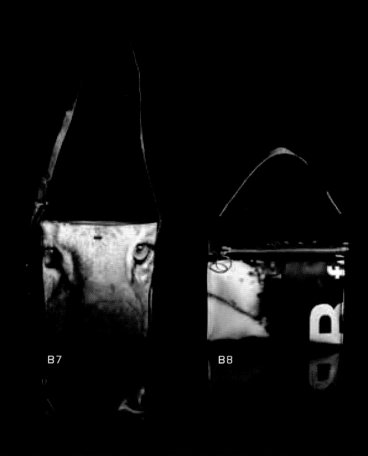

B7

B8

:: Day

B5

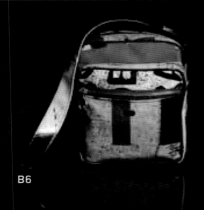

B6

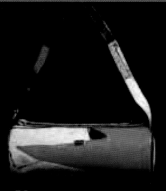

B2

B4

:: Day

:: Day

COMPLEMENTOS

SHAMPOO 30x16X9 cm
CASH 17,5x13,5x2 cm
KEY 11,5x5x4 cm
WALLY 9x13,5x2,5 cm
VISA 9x10x1 cm
CLICK 2x8 cm
MOBY 7x10,5x2 cm

Vaho Works

TOKIO FAMILY

1 TOKIO XL 37x32x10,5 cm
2 TOKIO L   27x32x7,5 cm
3 TOKIO M   28x26,5x7,5 cm
4 TOKIO S   22x27x7,5 cm

Vaho Works

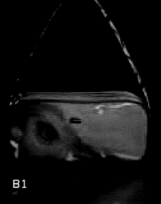

B1

B3

:: Day

RAVEL PACK
‹‹‹‹‹‹‹‹‹‹‹‹‹‹‹‹‹‹‹‹‹‹

1

NONE OF YOU
WILL EVER KNOW
MY INTENTIONS

13

:: Day

Flaya

Sixten

:: Day

152 Birgit Simons

153 Birgit Simons

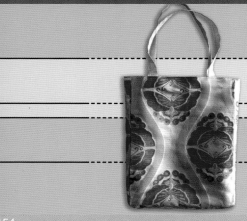

154   Birgit Simons

155   Birgit Simons

WITH LOVE

Andre Nossek - Via Grafik

:: Day

Hilnando Mendes

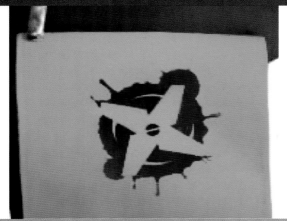

Hilnando Mendes

Diogo Paul

Diogo Paul

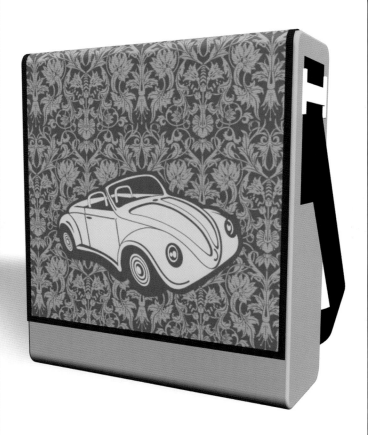

Diogo Paulo

Patrícia Toyama

:: Day

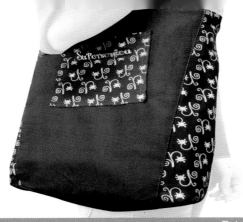

Patrícia Toyama

Patrícia Toyama

166

Andre Nossek - Via Grafi

167

Andre Nossek - Via Grafi

DESIRE IN RUINS

Andre Nossek - Via Grafik

118 :: 119

Elisabeth Dunker

:: Day

70   Elisabeth Dunker

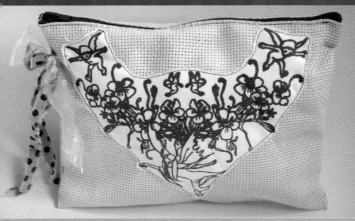

71   Elisabeth Dunker

172

173

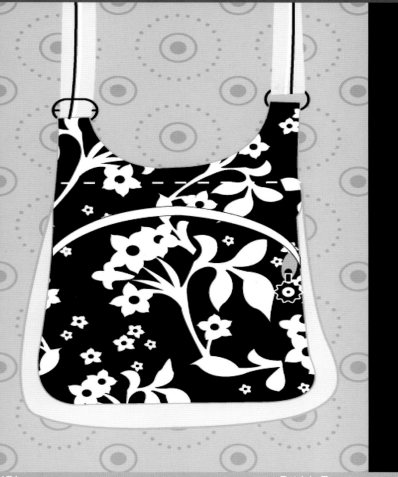

175   Andre Nossek - Via Grafik

:: Day

Shue Cane

Shue Cane

dona coisa

Cuca Design - Mariana Uchoa

dona coisa

Cuca Design - Mariana Uchoa

dona coisa

dona coisa

Cuca Design - Mariana Uchoa

126 :: 127

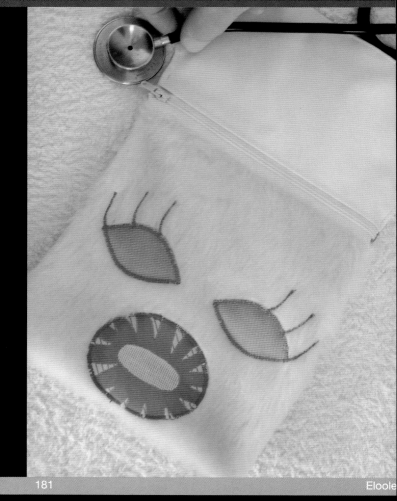

:: Day

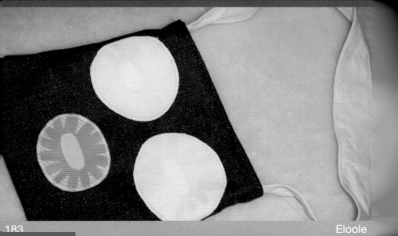

Felipe Borges - Original Handmade

Eloole

187

Patrícia Toyama

:: Day

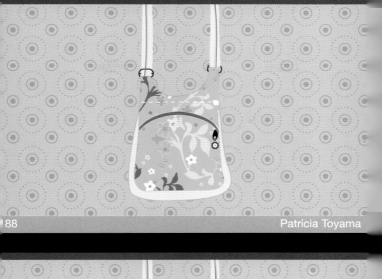

88   Patrícia Toyama

89   Patrícia Toyama

Patrícia Toyam

Patrícia Toyam

flôdipá

Patrícia Toyama

134 :: 135

Paula Salla

:: Day

Paula Sal

Paula Sal

Paula Salla

Sonia Souz

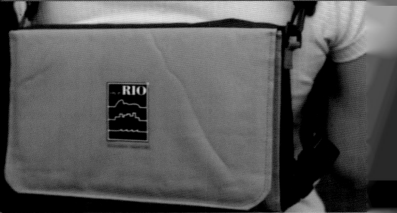

Sonia Souza

Sonia Souza

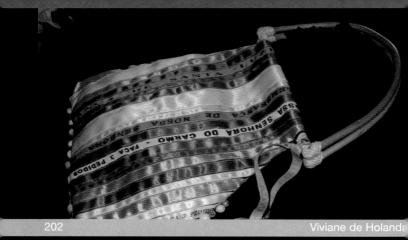

202   Viviane de Holanda

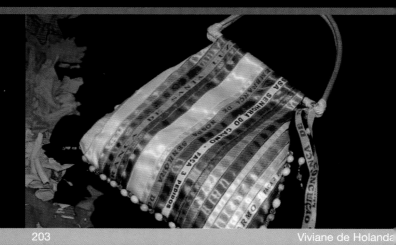

203   Viviane de Holanda

:: Day

NI
GH
T

A bag used for carrying money and small personal items or accessories (especially by women).

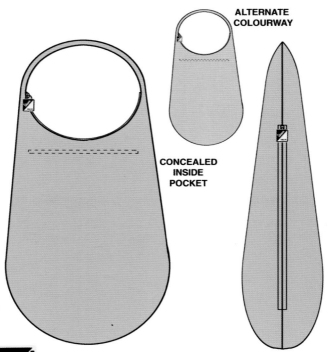

ALTERNATE COLOURWAY

CONCEALED INSIDE POCKET

FIRENZE SHOULDER BAG

SOFT CALFSKIN LEATHER

Pure Evil

:: Night

Allison Teich

Allison Teich

Thel

Thel

TOP VIEW

SIDE VIEW

**FULLY LINED
WITH INSIDE POCKET**

**ALTERNATE
COLOURWAY**

**MAGNETIC
STUD
CLOSURE**

'THE ITALIAN CONNECTION' BAG
FINEST QUALITY ITALIAN LEATHER WITH THICK TOPSTITCH

Allison Teich

:: Night

12   Marshall Trading

13   Allison Teich

Arturo Eler

Arturo Eler

Arturo Elena

:: Night

218

Arturo Elena

219

Arturo Elena

Arturo Elen

Arturo Elen

Arturo Elena

Daniella Zylbersztajn

:: Night

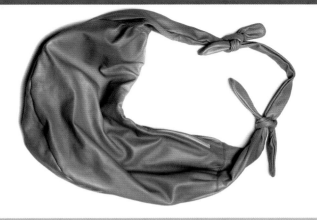

24

Daniella Zylbersztajn

25

Daniella Zylbersztajn

Daniella Zylberszta

Daniella Zylberszta

Daniella Zylbersztajn

Hardtroz

:: Night

Daniella Zylbersztajn

Daniella Zylbersztajn

Arturo Elen

Arturo Elen

Arturo Elena

164 :: 165

Maria Aparecida Silva Ribeiro

:: Night

Hardtroze

Maria Aparecida Silva Ribeiro

Roberta Montagno

Roberta Montagno

241   Roberta Montagno

:: Night

Roberta Montagnoli

Roberta Montagnoli

244   Vivi Tedesch

245   Vivi Tedesch

Vivi Tedeschi

 Vivi Tedeschi

:: Night

Vivi Tedeschi

Vivi Tedeschi

Vivi Tedesc

Vivi Tedesc

Sofia Dia

:: Night

Alzira & Lucio

Alzira & Lucio

256

257

Friederike Schaab

 Friederike Schaab

:: Night

60   Friederike Schaab

'61   Friederike Schaab

262   Friederike Schaa

263   Friederike Schaa

Friederike Schaab

184 :: 185

vicky

Felipe Borges - Original Handmade

:: Night

Felipe Borges - Original Handmade

sho

Felipe Borges - Original Handmade

268　　　　　　　　　　　　　　　　　　　　Jamille Ventur

269　　　　　　　　　　　　　　　　　　　　Paula Sall

Thelu

188 :: 189

Carina Sting

:: Night

Vitor Zanini Christino

Vitor Zanini Christino

DIF
FE
RE
NT

Different shapes and designs for any kind of use. Fun, serious, expensive or cheap.

Alessa

:: Different

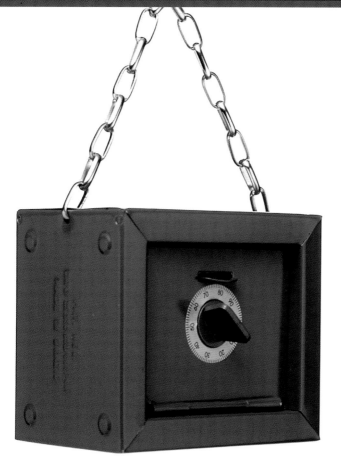

Aless

:: Different

Anabella Giorgi

Alessa

283   Christoph Seil

284   Christoph Seil

Christoph Seiler

200 :: 201

:: Different

87

Allison Teich

88

Allison Teich

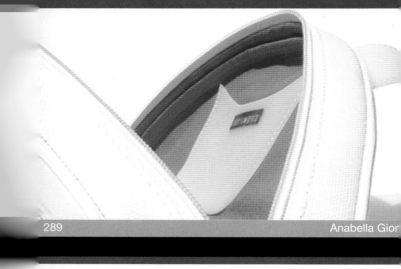

Anabella Gior

Anabella Gior

Diff

Anabella Giorgi

Juarez Escostegu

:: Different

Juarez Escosteguy

Juarez Escosteguy

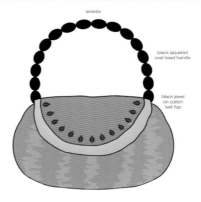

exterior

black laquered
oval bead handle

black jewel
on cotton
twill flap

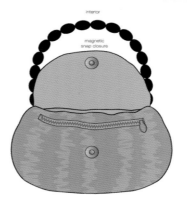

interior

magnetic
snap closure

Consanguineo

:: Different

Consanguineo

Consanguineo

Cozete Gelli - Sinhazinh

Daphne Seg

Consanguineo

:: Different

Consanguineo

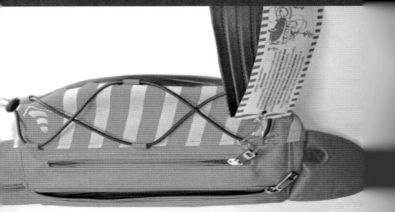
Consanguineo

Daphne Segal

216 :: 217

Hugo Muld

:: Different

IT'S A JUNGLE OUT THERE

04

Hugo Mulder

Hugo Mulder

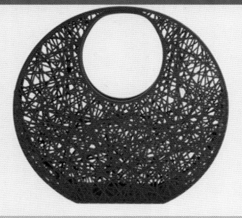

313   Roberta Montagno

314   Roberta Montagno

:: Different

Roberta Montagnoli

Roberta Montagno

:: Different

Roberta Montagnoli

Roberta Montagnoli

palm

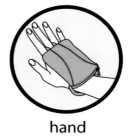

hand

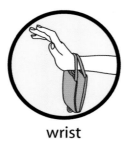

wrist

fingers

322   Ateliê Halo

323   Akihiro Sai

:: Different

Akihiro Sai

Karolina Wiewiorowska

:: Different

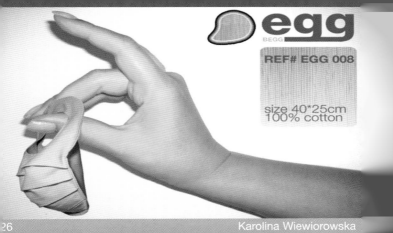

egg
BEGG

REF# EGG 008

size 40*25cm
100% cotton

Karolina Wiewiorowska

egg
BEGG

REF# EGG 009

size 40*25cm
felt

Karolina Wiewiorowska

328 Jamille Ventu

329 Susu Bac

Susu Bags

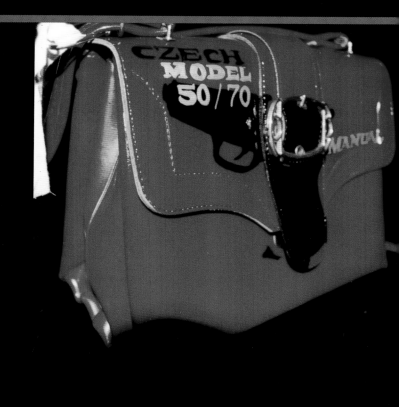

Naja Conrad

:: Different

hand
bag

Only for the future

:: Different

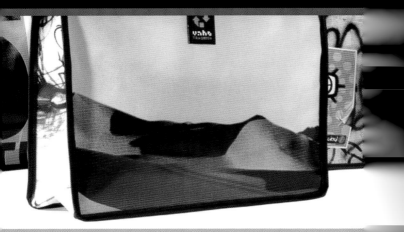

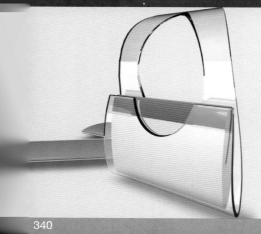

Daniel da Costa Lu

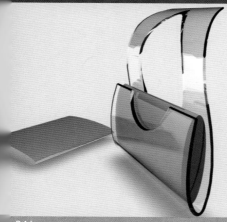

Daniel da Costa Lu

Daniel da Costa Luís

238 :: 239

:: Different

44   Atelie Halo

45   Atelie Halo

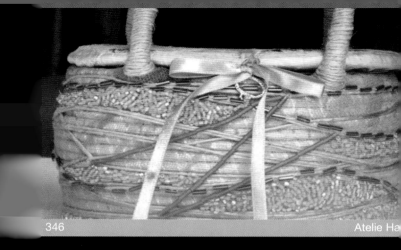
Atelie Ha

Atelie Ha

Atelie Halo

Daniel Freita

:: Different

350

Daniel Freitag

351

Daniel Freitag

352   Daniel Freita

353   Daniel Freita

Daniel Freitag

Daniel Freitag

:: Different

Daniel Freitag

Daniel Freitag

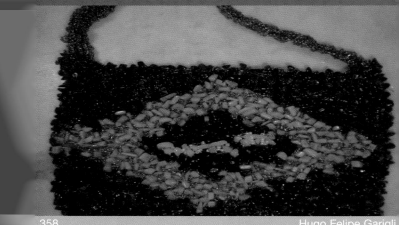

358   Hugo Felipe Garigli

359   Hugo Felipe Garigli

Hugo Felipe Gariglio

250 :: 251

Jamille Ventura

Jamille Ventura

:: Different

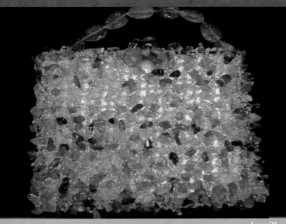

Jamille Ventura

Jamille Ventura

Marcio Gibra

Marcio Gibra

Marcio Gibram

254 :: 255

:: Different

Glitschka Studios

Natacha Kadhija

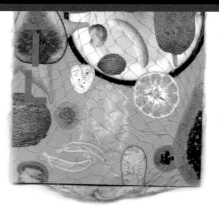

Wasted German Youth

PAPER

Sack: a bag made of paper or plastic used to hold customer purchases.

Squadra Diseño

:: Paper

Squadra Diseño

Squadra Diseño

THINK
ONLY
AFTER
YOU
HAVE
DONE IT

Elisabet Sol

THEY
STILL
DON'T
REALIZE
HOW
CRAZY
YOU ARE

Elisabet Sol

Lorinda Paganc

BLOOMSBURY
LONDON

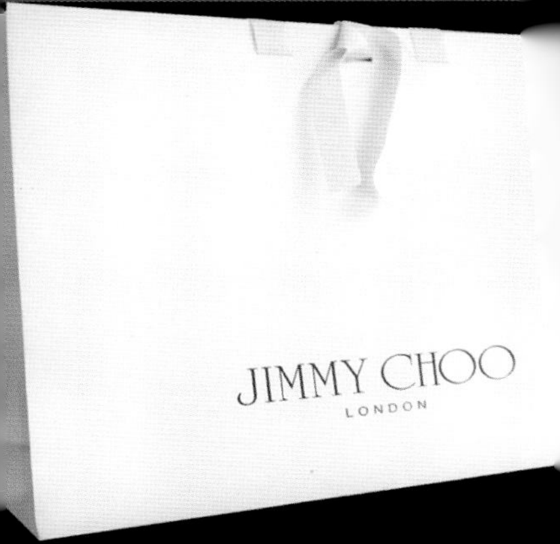

JIMMY CHOO
LONDON

Boris Ljubici

Boris Ljubici

Boris Ljubicic

268 :: 269

Lorinda Pagano

:: Paper

Thank You!
Thank You!
Thank You!

Love, Your Body

Thank You!
Thank You!
Thank You!

Love, Your Body

PART
ONE

edw
ard
huta
barat

www.edwardhutabarat.com

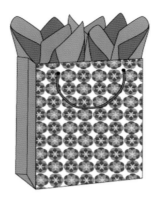

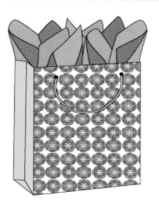

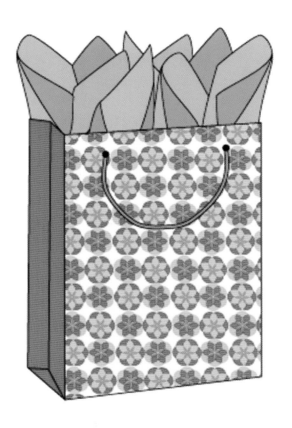

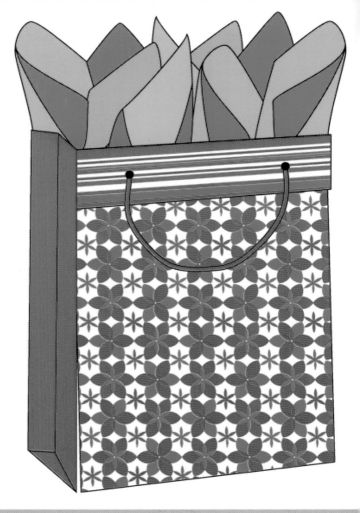

:: Paper

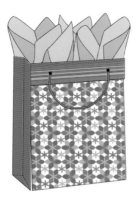

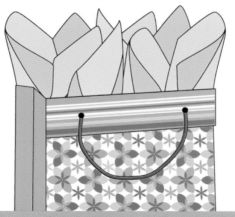

bliss

VIA MONTENAP...
MILANO

bliss

Anna Grimald...

Gelo

Corso Italia 18, Novara, telefono 0321 390122

Anna Grimald...

springtime is here.

DAVIDE CENCI

ROMA	MILANO	NEW YORK
via Campo Marzio, 1-7	via Manzoni, 7	801 Madison Avenue
Tel. 06-6990681	Tel. 02-8646232	Tel. 212-628991
	www.davidecenci.com	

ROMA
VIA CAMPO MARZIO 1-7
TEL. 06-699-0681

MILANO
VIA MANZONI 7
TEL. 02-864-65132

NEW YORK

Guilherme Sebastiany / Sebastiany Branding

Boris Ljubicic

Boris Ljubicic

Rico Lins + Studio

403   Jon Wippic

:: Paper

404   Aloof Design

405   Aloof Design

Squadra Diseño

Rico Lins + Studio

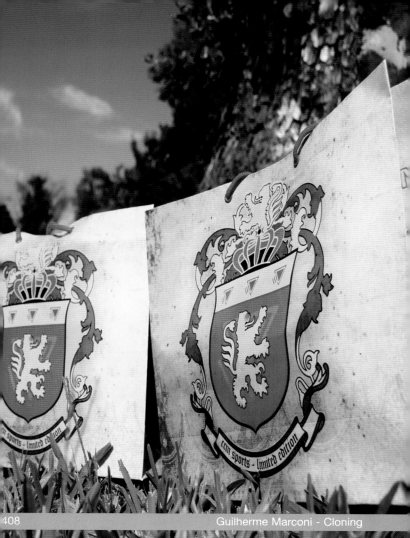

Guilherme Marconi - Cloning

:: Paper

JUBES is a high-fibre, low-calorie and cholesterol-free dessert. Spend hours of fun munching these chewy, juicy cubes or mix it with cocktails and other desserts to create your very own treats. Light and fibrous, it's especially suitable for the health conscious. Best of all, you can pick your choice of real tasty fun from six different flavours!

jubes
Nata De Coco

juicycubes.com

:: Paper

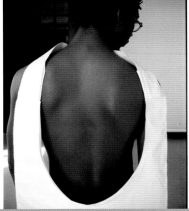

Krukurva

292 :: 293

 Nelson Araujo

:: Paper

Nelson Araujo

Nelson Araujo

Nando Corrêa - Berinjela Desig

Nando Corrêa - Berinjela Desig

Nando Corrêa - Berinjela Design

WWW.BIOMONDEGO.PT

Biomondego

427
Adriano Esteves

:: Paper

Adriano Esteves

Adriano Esteves

Adriano Esteves

Adriano Esteves

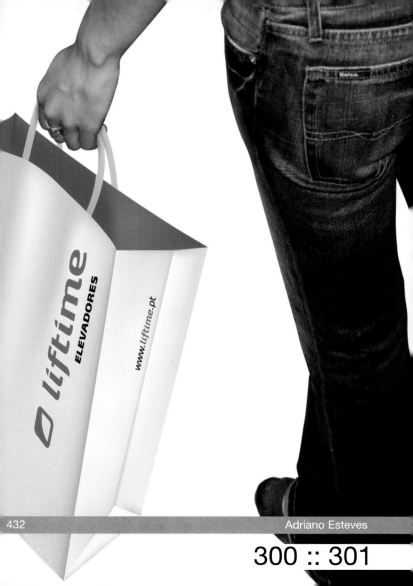

liftime
ELEVADORES

www.liftime.pt

Adriano Esteves

300 :: 301

:: Paper

Simon Farrow

Flavio de Almeida Hobo

Sensual

Emanuel Barbosa

438

Emanuel Barbosa

304 :: 305

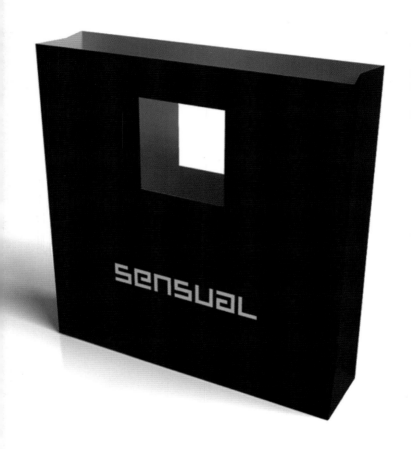

:: Paper

440   Squadra Diseño

441   Squadra Diseño

Andre Nossek - Via Grafik

Andre Nossek - Via Grafik

:: Paper

Andre Nossek - Via Grafik

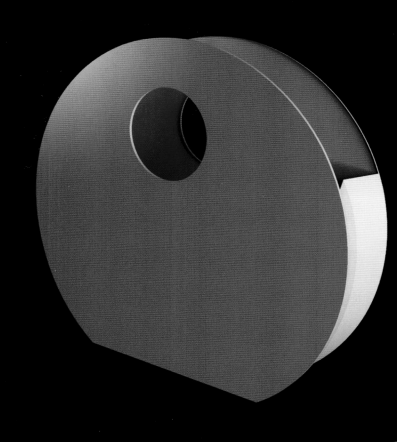

Sensual

:: Paper

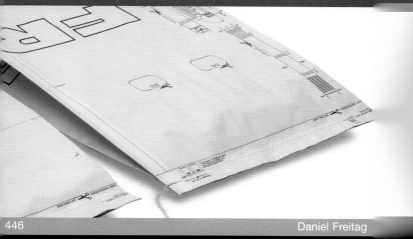

Daniel Freitag

Daniel Freitag

Arturo Elena

449

Agustin Valca

Normai Lai

:: Paper

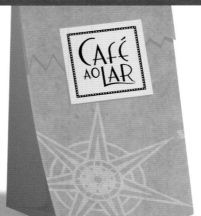

Guilherme Sebastiany / Sebastiany Branding

Sonsoles Llorens

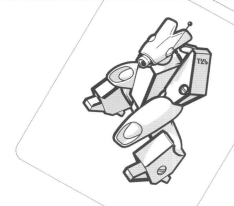

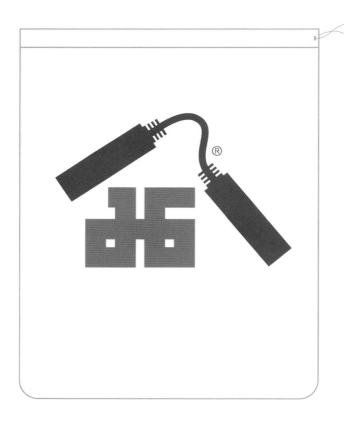

:: Plastic

Segura-Inc

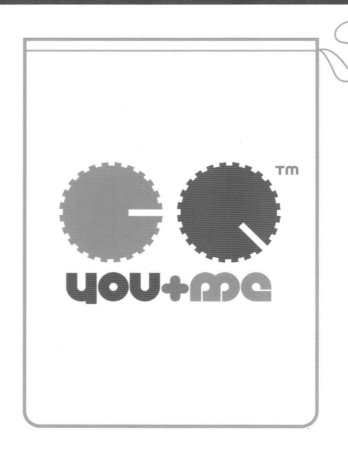

Segura-Inc

:: Plastic

WWW.T26.COM

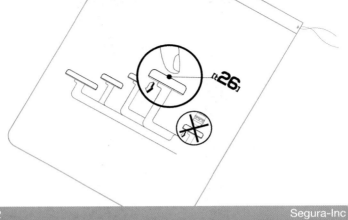

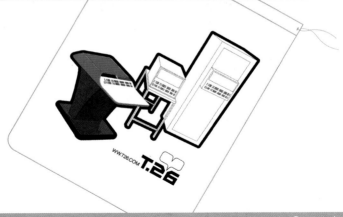

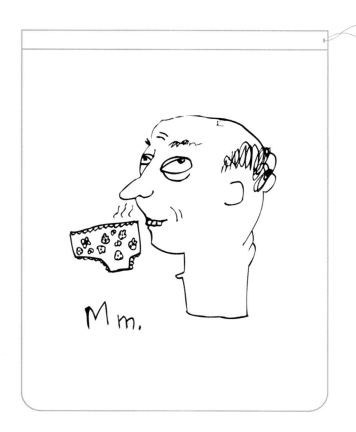

Segura-Inc

segura inc presents

tokyo

segura inc presents

tokyo

T-26 DIGITAL TYPE FOUNDRY
1110 NORTH MILWAUKEE AVENUE
FIRST FLOOR, CHICAGO, ILLINOIS
60622, 4007 USA
1.800.T26 FONT [US TOLL FREE]
TELEPHONE: 773.862.1201
FACSIMILE: 773.862.1214
E-MAIL: INFO@T26.COM
WEB: WWW.T26.COM

01.04.01
THRU 25.04.01
TDC EXHIBITION AT THE GINZA
GRAPHIC GALLERY

05.04.01
OPENING PARTY AND
THE AWARD PRESENTATION
CEREMONY

07.04.01
LECTURE AT THE GALLERIA
HALL IN THE TOKYO DESIGN
CENTER

you+me

01.04.01
THRU 25.04.01
TDC EXHIBITION AT THE GINZA
GRAPHIC GALLERY

07.04.01
LECTURE AT THE
TOKYO DESIGN
CENTER

you+me

475

Segura-Inc

:: Plastic

Segura-Inc

Segura-Inc

Segura-Inc

Segura-Inc

Simon Farrow

:: Plastic

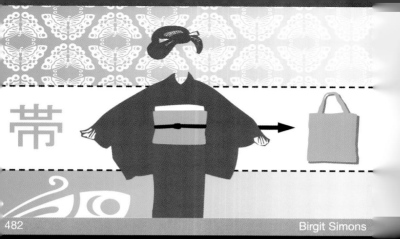

482

Birgit Simons

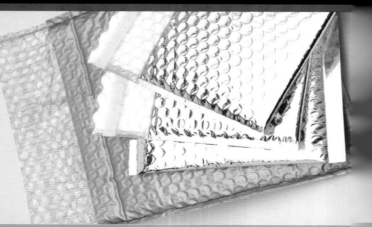

483

Simon Farrow

Simon Farrow

Design.
Miami/ Basel

4040 NE 2nd Avenue, Suite 404,
Miami, Florida 33137 USA
Call 1.305.572.0866 Fax 1.305.572.0864
Email: info@designmiami.com
www.designmiami.com

Pure Evil

plant

VEGETARIAN · FOOD · DRINK

PLANT TRAY

BREAKFAST LUNCH

SANDWICHES SALADS

SOUPS CAKES BREADS

COFFEE TEA

SMOOTHIES JUICES

41 Poland Street W1 T 020 7734 7528
www.plantfooddrink.com

Simon Farrow

LUNAR MAP

MOON
ESTATES

ONE ACRE LUNAR DEED/.
LUNAR CONSTITUTION/LUNAR MAP/.
PERSONALISATION AND REGISTRATION/.
MINERAL RIGHTS/.
DECLARATION OF OWNERSHIP.

MOON
ESTATES

MoonE... ...m Ltd
Freepost (S...
St.Austell PL26
United Kingdom
Planet Earth
...estates.com
...ephone orders, 080...

Simon Farrow

:: Plastic

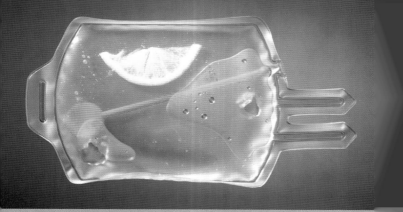

488   Simon Farrow

489   Adriano Esteves

Say that you love me!

Nice Lopes

342 :: 343

:: Plastic

Urban Dance

¹hip *adj* **hip•per; hip• pest:** keenly aware of or interested in the newest developments or styles.

Nice Lopes

Nice Lopes

DIRECTORY

I am very grateful to everyone who has
participated in this book. I would like to thank
all of the designers and graphic studios who have
collaborated on this project.

Without these individuals, this project
would never have been possible:
-

Adriana Jordan
Antoni Canal
Isabel Lorente
Pamela Santacroce
Sylvie Estrada
-

For all my students at the Instituto Europeo di Design, Barcelona

Mito
Branding Design

Mix 4 spoonfuls of design, 3 of branding and 2 copywriters together in a pan and you'll get Mito Design, an insights and solutions firm that will give you the exact roadmap to get you where you want to go. Our goal is to achieve complete customer satisfaction. Whether your needs are conservative or ambitious, we will give you everything we've got to make this experience an unforgettable one.

Good luck!

www.mitodesign.com